JOHN THOMPSON'S
EASIEST PIANO COURSE

FIRST CHRISTMAS DUETS

ISBN 978-1-4234-9520-8

EXCLUSIVELY DISTRIBUTED BY

WILLIS MUSIC

HAL•LEONARD®
CORPORATION
7777 W. BLUEMOUND RD. P.O. BOX 13819
MILWAUKEE, WISCONSIN 53213

Visit Hal Leonard Online at
www.halleonard.com

Teachers and Parents

This collection of popular Christmas duets, arranged in the John Thompson tradition, is intended as supplementary material for the elementary level pianist. The duets may also be used for sight-reading practice by more advanced students.

CONTENTS

Believe

from Warner Bros. Pictures' THE POLAR EXPRESS

SECONDO

Words and Music by Glen Ballard
and Alan Silvestri
Arranged by Carolyn Miller

Play both hands one octave lower.

Believe

from Warner Bros. Pictures' THE POLAR EXPRESS

PRIMO

Words and Music by Glen Ballard
and Alan Silvestri
Arranged by Carolyn Miller

Play both hands one octave higher.

SECONDO

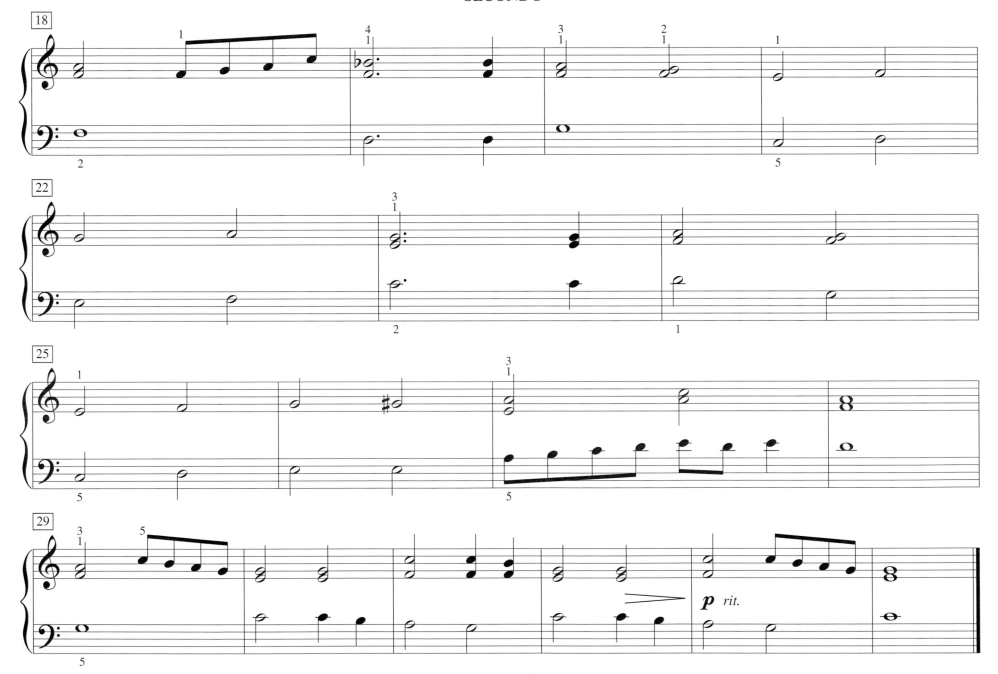

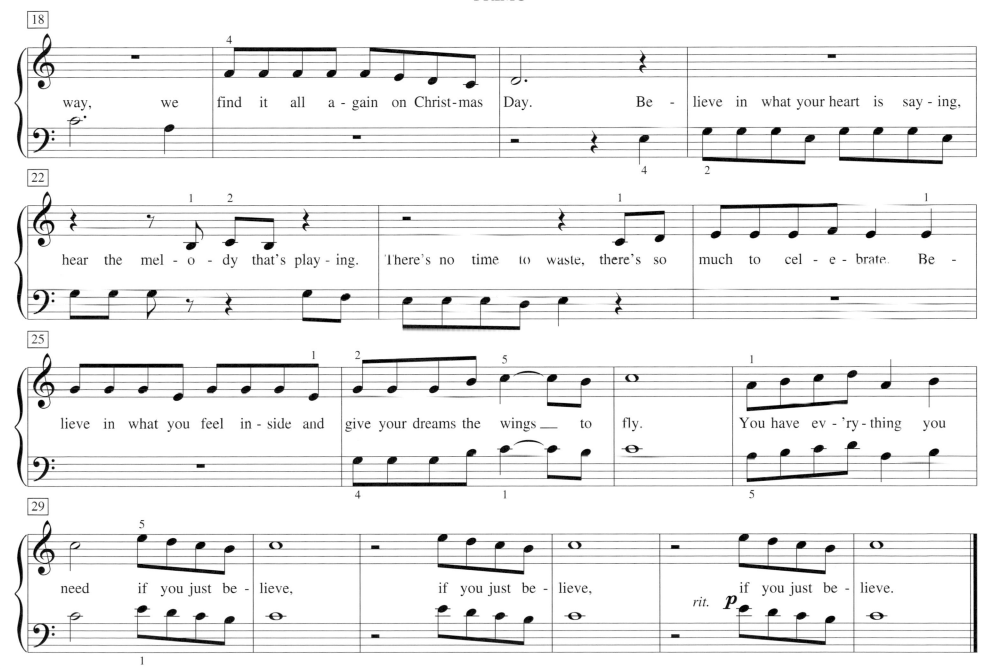

C-H-R-I-S-T-M-A-S

SECONDO

Words by Jenny Lou Carson
Music by Eddy Arnold
Arranged by Carolyn Miller

Play both hands one octave lower.

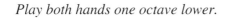

C-H-R-I-S-T-M-A-S

PRIMO

Words by Jenny Lou Carson
Music by Eddy Arnold
Arranged by Carolyn Miller

Play both hands as written.

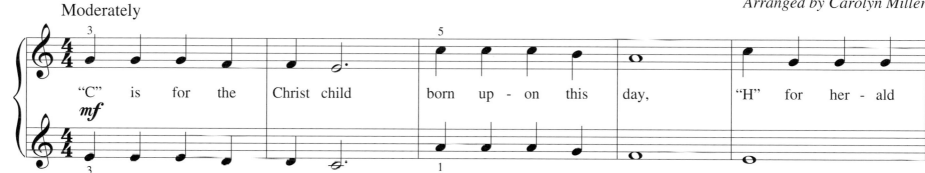

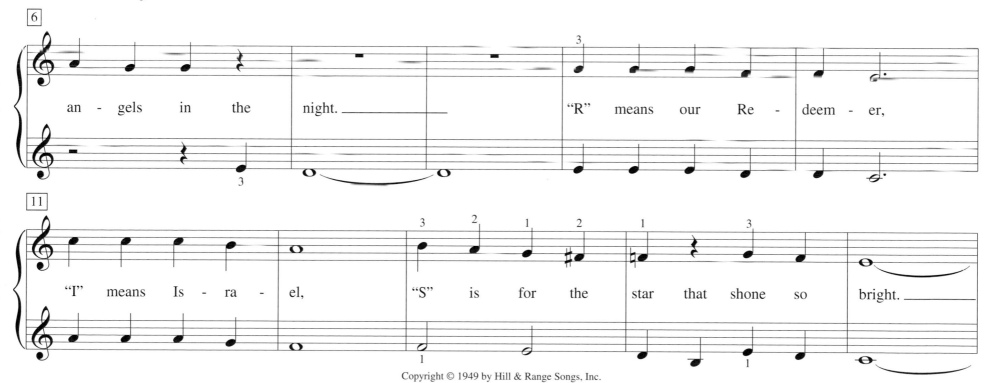

SECONDO

PRIMO

Do You Hear What I Hear

SECONDO

Words and Music by Noel Regney
and Gloria Shayne
Arranged by Carolyn Miller

Play both hands as written.

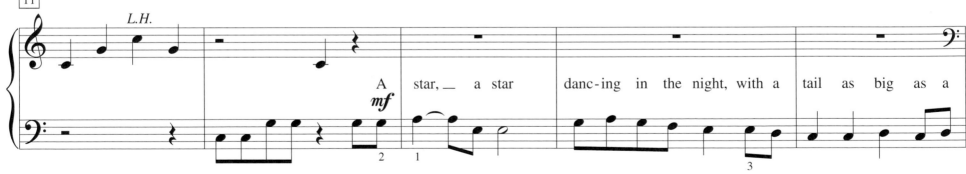

Do You Hear What I Hear

PRIMO

Words and Music by Noel Regney
and Gloria Shayne
Arranged by Carolyn Miller

Play both hands one octave higher.

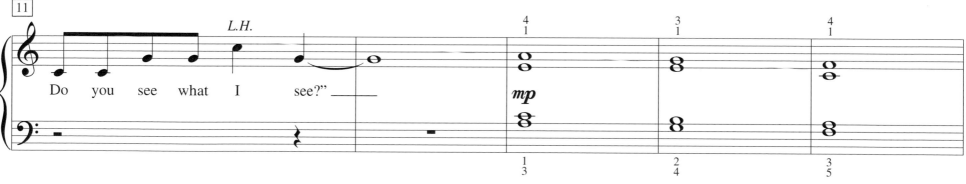

SECONDO

SECONDO

Frosty the Snow Man

SECONDO

Words and Music by Steve Nelson
and Jack Rollins
Arranged by Carolyn Miller

Play both hands one octave lower.

Lively, with a lilt

Frosty the Snow Man

PRIMO

Words and Music by Steve Nelson
and Jack Rollins
Arranged by Carolyn Miller

Play both hands one octave higher.

Lively, with a lilt

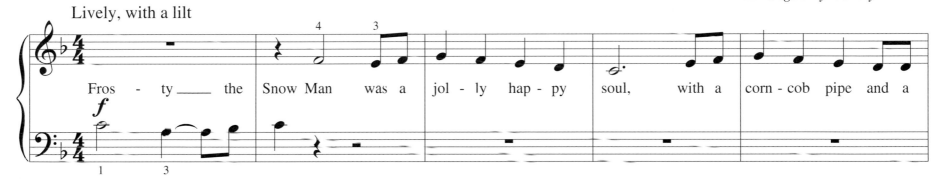

Fros - ty ____ the Snow Man was a jol - ly hap - py soul, with a corn - cob pipe and a

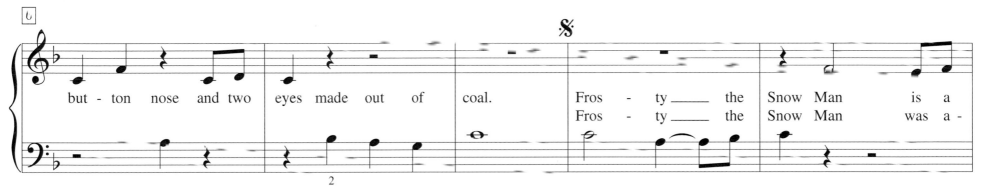

but - ton nose and two eyes made out of coal. Fros - ty ____ the Snow Man is a
Fros - ty ____ the Snow Man was a-

fair - y tale, they say. He was made of snow, but the chil - dren know how he came to life one
live as he could be, and the chil - dren say he could laugh and play just the same as you and

To Coda

SECONDO

*tap knuckles on fallboard

PRIMO

*tap L.H. knuckles on fallboard

Here Comes Santa Claus
(Right Down Santa Claus Lane)

SECONDO

Words and Music by Gene Autry
and Oakley Haldeman
Arranged by Carolyn Miller

Play both hands one octave lower.

Here Comes Santa Claus

(Right Down Santa Claus Lane)

PRIMO

Words and Music by Gene Autry
and Oakley Haldeman
Arranged by Carolyn Miller

Play both hands one octave higher.

Here comes San - ta Claus! Here comes San - ta Claus! Right down San - ta Claus Lane!

Vix - en and Blitz - en and all his rein - deer are pull - ing on the rein.
He's got a bag that is filled with toys for the boys and girls a - gain.

Bells are ring - ing, chil - dren sing - ing, all is mer - ry and bright. Hang your stock - ings and
Hear those sleigh - bells jin - gle - jan - gle, what a beau - ti - ful sight! Jump in bed, cov - er

SECONDO

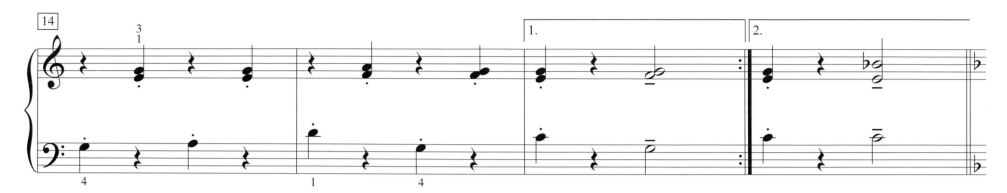

Here comes San - ta Claus! Here comes San - ta Claus! Right down San - ta Claus Lane!

He does - n't care if you're rich or poor, he loves you just the same.

PRIMO

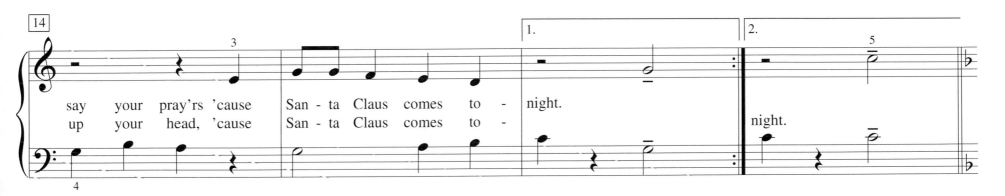

say   your   pray'rs 'cause   San - ta   Claus   comes   to -   night.
up   your   head, 'cause   San - ta   Claus   comes   to -   night.

San - ta   knows   that

SECONDO

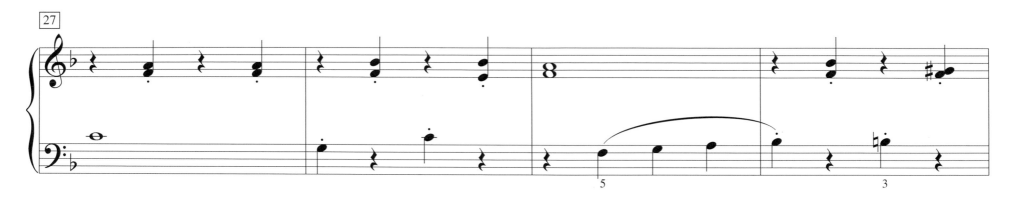

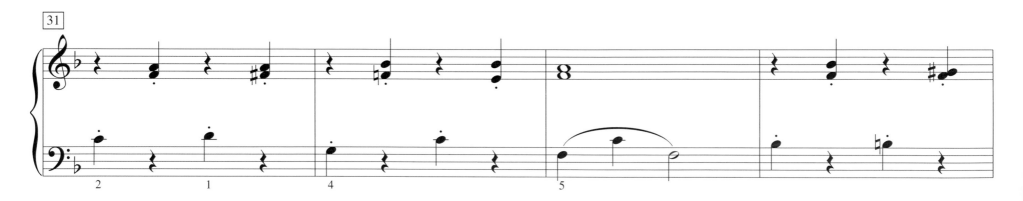

San - ta Claus comes to-... San - ta Claus comes to - night!

PRIMO

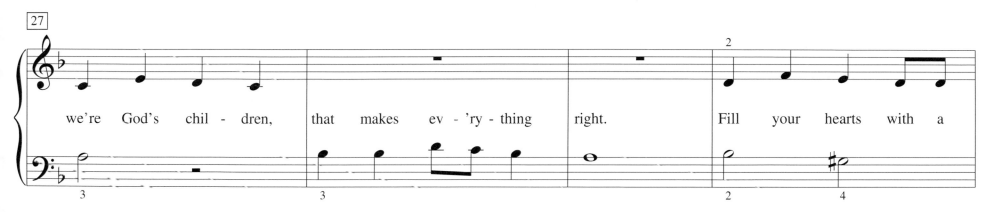

we're God's chil - dren, that makes ev - 'ry - thing right. Fill your hearts with a

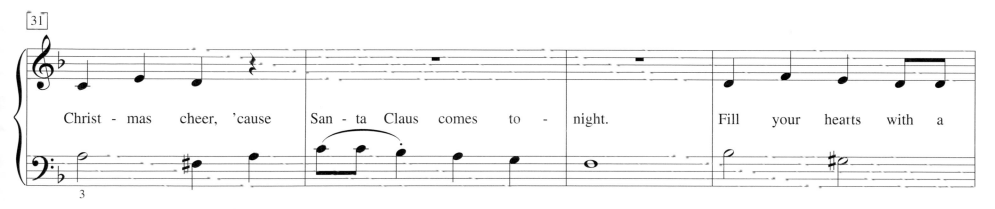

Christ - mas cheer, 'cause San - ta Claus comes to - night. Fill your hearts with a

Christ - mas cheer, 'cause San - ta Claus comes to-... San - ta Claus comes to - night!

I Saw Mommy Kissing Santa Claus

SECONDO

Words and Music by Tommie Connor
Arranged by Carolyn Miller

Play both hands one octave lower.

Moderately

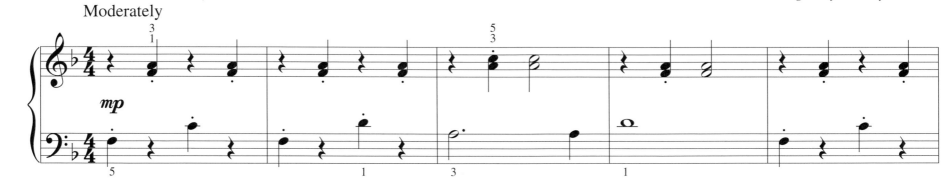

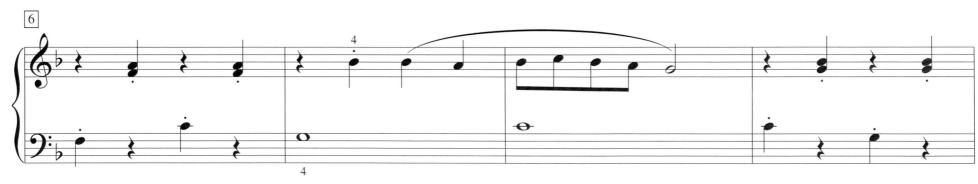

I Saw Mommy Kissing Santa Claus

PRIMO

Words and Music by Tommie Connor
Arranged by Carolyn Miller

Play both hands one octave higher.

Moderately

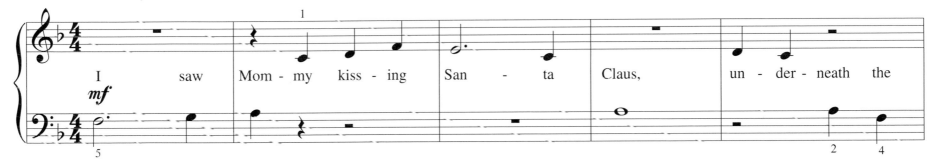

SECONDO

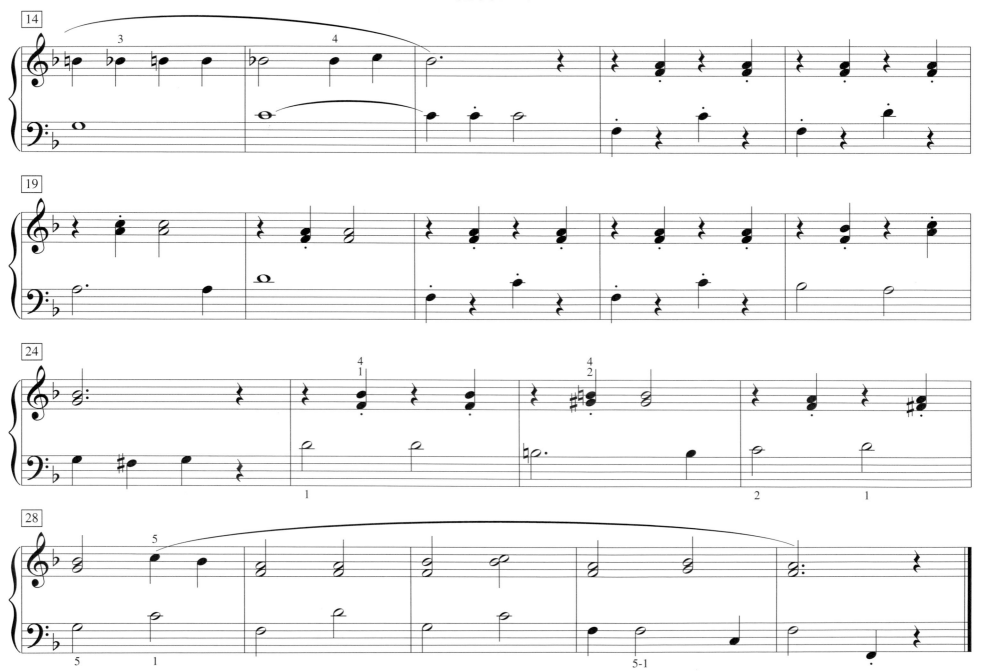

PRIMO

The Most Wonderful Day of the Year

SECONDO

Play both hands one octave lower.

Music and Lyrics by Johnny Marks
Arranged by Carolyn Miller

The Most Wonderful Day of the Year

PRIMO

Play both hands one octave higher.

Music and Lyrics by Johnny Marks
Arranged by Carolyn Miller

SECONDO

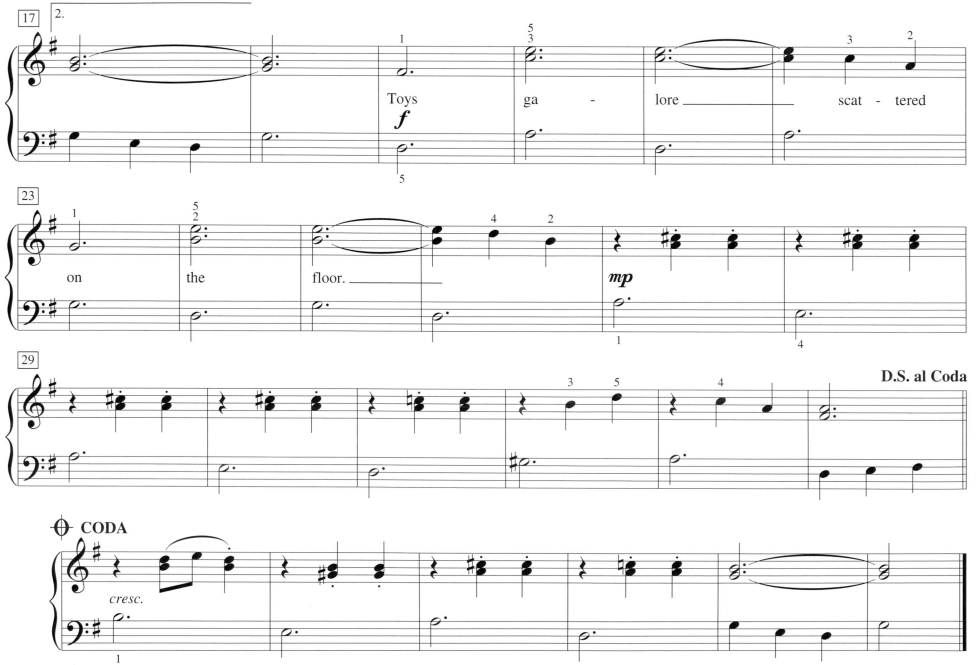

PRIMO

Nuttin' for Christmas

SECONDO

Words and Music by Roy Bennett
and Sid Tepper
Arranged by Carolyn Miller

Play both hands one octave lower.

Moderately, with regret

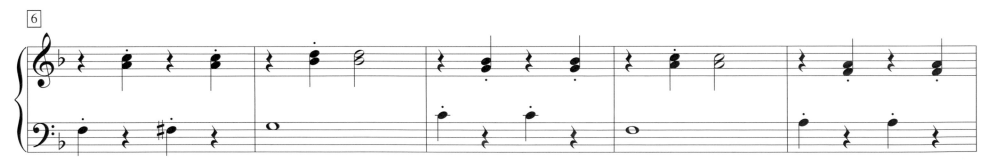

I'm get - tin' nut - tin' for Christ - mas,

Nuttin' for Christmas

PRIMO

Words and Music Roy Bennett
and Sid Tepper
Arranged by Carolyn Miller

Play both hands one octave higher.

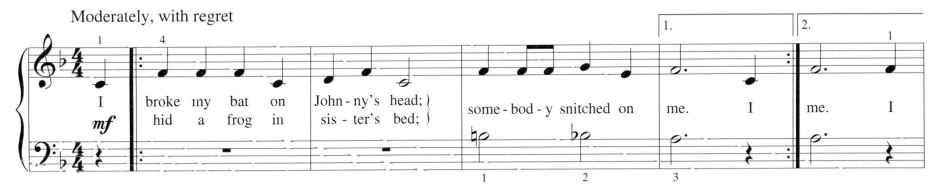

Moderately, with regret

I broke my bat on John-ny's head; hid a frog in sis-ter's bed; some-bod-y snitched on me. I me. I

spilled some ink on Mom-my's rug; I made Tom-my eat a bug; bought some gum with a

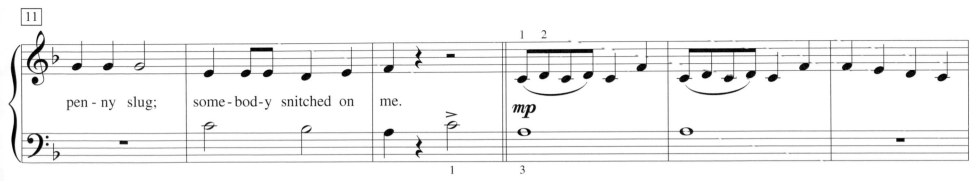

pen-ny slug; some-bod-y snitched on me.

mp

SECONDO

EASIEST PIANO COURSE
Supplementary Songbooks

Fun repertoire books are available as an integral part of **John Thompson's Easiest Piano Course**. Graded to work alongside the course, these pieces are ideal for pupils reaching the end of Part 2. They are invaluable for securing basic technique as well as developing musicality and enjoyment.

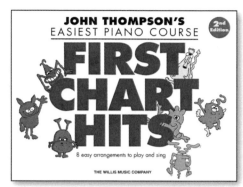

John Thompson's Easiest Piano Course

00414014 Part 1 – Book only $6.99
00414018 Part 2 – Book only $6.99
00414019 Part 3 – Book only $7.99
00414112 Part 4 – Book only $7.99

First Beethoven *arr. Hussey*
00171709 .... $7.99

First Chart Hits – 2nd Edition
00289560 .... $9.99

First Disney Songs *arr. Miller*
00416880 .... $9.99

Also available:

First Children's Songs *arr. Hussey*
00282895 .... $7.99

First Classics
00406347 .... $6.99

First Disney Favorites *arr. Hussey*
00319587 .... $9.99

First Mozart *arr. Hussey*
00171851 .... $7.99

First Nursery Rhymes
00406229 .... $6.99

First Worship Songs *arr. Austin*
00416892 .... $8.99

First Jazz Tunes *arr. Baumgartner*
00120872 .... $7.99

First Pop Songs *arr. Miller*
00416954 .... $8.99

First Showtunes *arr. Hussey*
00282907 .... $9.99